Nature activity book

Published by the Natural History Museum, London

Contents

Nature is everywhere

Our gardens and parks are amazing places to discover wildlife and experience nature, and you'll find lots of ideas throughout this book to keep you busy.

Why do bees make honey?

To feed the baby bees in their hives. They make extra honey to eat throughout winter.

What's all the fuss about worms?

These little wigglers help keep our soil healthy. They eat their way through dead leaves and move nutrients through the soil so plants can grow.

Where can I find a tadpole?

In a pond or stream in springtime, where there aren't many fish (fish eat tadpoles!). They start as little jelly eggs and hatch about three weeks after being laid. Always put tadpoles back into the same place you found them.

Where do clouds come from?

Clouds are made in the sky when tiny water droplets gather together. The droplets are so small and light that they can float in the air.

Where do butterflies lay their eggs?

They lay them on or near the plant that their babies, which hatch into little hungry caterpillars, want to eat.

What do plants eat?

Plants are very clever because they make their own food using just sunlight and water. This is called photosynthesis.

Why do some trees lose their leaves?

Because in the winter there's not enough light or warmth for leaves, so trees have a rest and wait for spring to come.

Keep a wildlife diary

Why not begin your nature journey with a wildlife diary – it's a great way to get to know the seasons and the wildlife around you.

Use a blank book and write the date and where you are at the top of each page before you record anything. Here are some ideas to get you started.

Describe the weather you see from your bedroom window before you get up.

List all the birds that you see while you're eating breakfast, and then draw them.

Press your favourite flowers between the pages as a keepsake. Remember to make a note of the names of your flowers, where you found them and the date.

How about taking your diary with you next time you go on a walk and record what you see and find.

Lift up a log or rock and list the insects you see before they scuttle away.

If you spot lots of downy feathers on the ground, there could be a nest nearby. Stick a feather in your diary and try and find out what bird it belongs to.

If you find nibbled fruit and nut shells a squirrel may have had a feast recently. Write down what fruit and nuts you find.

Fill your diary with...

Where is the best place to pick blackberries?

How many snails can you spot in one day?

Listen out for different animal sounds at night.

What creatures come into your home,
and in which seasons?

Make a list of the animals you see on your next walk.

Adopt a tree in your local park or street
and record how it changes
throughout the year.

Write a poem about nature.

Go explore

Head outdoors and start discovering.
What can you hear? What can
you see? What can you smell?

Whether it's spring, summer, autumn
or winter – there's lots to see and do!

SUMMER

Imitate the
sounds that
you hear.

SPRING

Look for different colours and
textures in nature. Rub your
hands over as many different
tree trunks as you can.
Are they bumpy,
rough or smooth?

Spot seasonal signs such
as spring and summer
blossom, new leaves and
berries appearing.

How many insects can
you find on one plant?

Count the petals on
flower heads.

AUTUMN

What is happening to the trees?

What's the smallest and biggest leaf that you can catch?

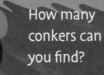

How many conkers can you find?

WINTER

Listen out for birds – they'll still be singing whatever the weather.

Look for animal shaped clouds.

And remember, you don't have to stay indoors when it's cold and wet. Wrap up warm and step outside!

Bird spotting

The colourful **blue tit** has a bright blue cap and yellow chest. This little bird regularly shows off its acrobatic skills as it feeds from birdfeeders and blackberry bushes.

Robins have a bright red breast and you can spot them all year round. If you spend lots of time digging outside, you may find one hopping around your wellies, looking for grubs.

Starlings are one of the noisiest garden birds! They look black from a distance but when you get closer their snowflake feathers sparkle with purples and greens.

Watch out for a flash of the shimmering blue cloak and satsuma orange chest of the **kingfisher** as it darts along the riverbank. These tiny birds have a high-pitched whistle call – listen out for it when you are next by a river.

At night you might hear the call of the **tawny owl**. In autumn and winter, the males make a 'to-wit' sound and the females hoot back with a 'to-woo'.

Male and female **blackbirds** are often spotted together, flipping fallen leaves searching for food, or at the other end of an earthworm. The males are black with a bright yellow beak and eye-ring, and females are speckled brown.

13

Leaf animals

When you're next out for a walk, look for fallen leaves. Collect some up and see what you can make – they might suddenly become a hedgehog, squirrel, fox or dinosaur.

Willow leaves are long and thin.

Beech leaves are oval and have jagged edges.

Pine needles are very thin leaves with a sharp pointy end.

Horse chestnut leaves are made up of 5 to 7 leaflets.

If you don't have any leaves, you can cut leaf shapes out of paper.

Oak leaves have rounded, wavy edges.

15

Build a bug hotel

Try making a bug hotel. Animals take time to get used to a new place and may not move in straight away. Check back after a few days to see if any creepy-crawlies have found somewhere safe to live.

You can use anything to build a bug hotel. Here are some suggestions:

Terracotta plant pots (whole and broken)

Bricks

Small planks of wood

Logs and twigs

Bamboo canes

Leaves

Moss

Pine cones

Conkers

Stones

1 Scout your outside space for a quiet, sheltered spot.

2 Place planks of wood on top of old bricks and put plant pots on top of them to make different levels.

3 Pick up pine cones, conkers or twigs on your next walk. Using the different things you have collected, fill up your hotel – this will help to attract all kinds of creatures. You can have lots of fun with your design.

4 Putting stones and broken plant pots on the bottom level of your hotel makes a cool shady spot for toads, slugs or snails.

Solitary bees like living alone. If you fill part of your hotel with short bamboo canes you might see a few buzzing around.

Make a hedgehog house

Our spikey friends are less common than they used to be, so give them somewhere safe to rest and sleep.

Keep the entrance clear at all times so your hedgehog can come and go easily.

WELCON

Hedgehogs mainly eat insects, worms, caterpillars and berries.

For your hedgehog house you need:

An adult's help

A quiet spot

For the large box – six pieces of untreated wood (two short sides, two long sides, a top and a bottom)

For the entrance tunnel – five smaller pieces of untreated wood (two long sides, a front, a top and a bottom)

Hammer, nails and wood glue

Two metal hinges

Dry leaves, straw and newspaper

Leaves, moss and sticks

1 To make the large box, cut a hedgehog-sized hole into one short side, about 13 cm by 13 cm. Then nail all the pieces of wood together to form a box with a base and hinged lid. The hinged lid means you can easily clean your box out between late March and early April – but only if it doesn't have a hedgehog in it!

2 To make the entrance tunnel, cut another hedgehog-sized hole into the front piece of wood. Nail all the pieces of wood together to form a tunnel. Glue the open end to the large box, placing it in front of the other hole. The tunnel prevents predators such as foxes from getting to the hedgehog with their paws.

3 Fill the box with straw, newspaper and dry leaves to keep the hedgehog cosy. There needs to be enough room for bedding and for the hedgehog to move around.

4 Find a safe quiet spot to put your hedgehog house in, and camouflage it with leaves and sticks.

Build a mini wildlife pond

Wildlife ponds are one of the best ways to attract wildlife. Choose a spot that gets a mixture of sun and shade during the day.

Here's what you need to get started:

A watertight container – is there anything you can upcycle? Maybe an old washing up bowl.

Old bricks, pebbles or bits of wood.

Pond plants – it's good to have at least one submerged plant, like hornwort, to oxygenate the water, and a floating flowering plant, such as frogbit. The more plant variety the better.

What wildlife can you find in your pond?

Pond plants

Willow moss
Water starwort
Water mint
Lesser spearwort
Greater bird's-foot trefoil
Water forget-me-not
Creeping Jenny
Water avens

1 Once you've found the perfect spot, dig a hole deep enough for your container and put it in the hole so the top of the container is level with the ground.

2 Use old bricks, pebbles or bits of wood to build a gentle slope at one end of your container so that creatures can climb in and out.

3 Fill your pond with rainwater. If you use tap water, leave it to stand for a few days so any chemicals evaporate.

4 Add a few pond plants and you'll be surprised at how quickly wildlife comes.

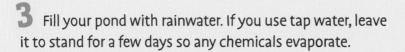

Birds will visit your mini pond to drink and wash in.

How to make a butterfly feeder

In summer when it's warm and dry, butterflies flutter around flowers looking for nectar to drink and leaves to lay their eggs on. You can help attract them with a butterfly feeder.

You will need:

Card

Colouring pencils

Scissors

Old plastic drink bottle top

Sticky tape

Glue

Cotton wool

Sugar

Water

Pot with soil in it

1 Draw a flower on your card and colour it in using bright colours, then cut it out.

2 Stick the flat side of your bottle top in the centre of your flower.

3 Use sticky tape to attach a pencil to the back of your flower.

4 Now stand your flower in the pot of soil and place outside.

5 Mix the sugar with some water and soak your cotton wool in it. Give your cotton wool a gentle squeeze and pop it inside the bottle top.

6 Watch for butterflies to flutter by, land and feed.

23

Make a pitfall trap

Making a pitfall trap is an excellent way to find insects and take a closer look at them.

You will need:

A trowel

An empty glass jar – make sure it's clean and isn't sticky inside

Bait – petals, leaves or fruit

A piece of wood to cover your pot

Stones

1 Dig a hole the size of your pot in the ground and put the pot in it.

2 Make sure the top of the pot is level with the ground and fill any gaps around the edge of the pot with soil.

3 Put your bait into the pot to attract your tiny visitors.

4 Add a few stones either side and place the piece of wood on top of them to stop the rain getting in.

5 Leave your trap for a few hours, then come back to see what you have. Make a note in your diary.

6 When you've finished with your trap, pack it away and fill your hole.

Give a bat a safe place to roost

All British bats eat insects, so plant flowers that give off scent at night, like honeysuckle and white jasmine, to attract night-flying insects. When they come, the bats will follow, flitting around looking for an insect-meal.

You will need:

Help from an adult

Untreated rough timber

Tape measure and pencil

Saw, hammer, nails and brackets

Autumn is the best time to install your box. It will give bats somewhere safe to sleep during the day.

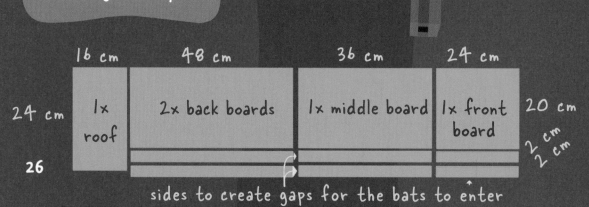

	16 cm	48 cm	36 cm	24 cm	
24 cm	1× roof	2× back boards	1× middle board	1× front board	20 cm

2 cm
2 cm

sides to create gaps for the bats to enter

Never disturb a bat box once it's up – look for droppings on the ground instead. All bat species and their roosts are now legally protected.

1 Mark and cut your timber to the dimensions shown.

2 Nail the two back boards together and use the sides of wood to create the entrance space in between the boards.

3 Then nail the middle board and its sides to the back board. Then nail the front board and its sides to the middle board.

4 Nail the roof in place. Make sure the back of the roof sits in line with the back of the box.

5 Attach your brackets to the back of your box and fix it as high as possible on a tree or the side of a building.

Plant a pollinator pot

To help attract insect pollinators like bees and butterflies, plant native wildflowers for them to visit. They will love these flowers and so will you.

You will need:

A pot with a hole in the bottom

Tray

Pebbles

Soil mix (half soil and half peat-free compost)

Native wildflower seeds

1 Place some pebbles at the bottom of your pot – this helps the water to drain.

2 Add your soil mix, leaving 2.5 cm at the top, saving some to cover the seeds.

3 Scatter your seeds over the soil and then sprinkle more soil over them and pat down firmly.

4 Water your pot but stop before the soil gets soggy.

5 Put your pot somewhere sunny and remember to water it regularly.

6 Wait for your flowers to grow!

Bees can see purple flowers more clearly than any other colour.

Feed the birds

Putting food out for birds is an easy thing to do and can help them survive, especially during the cold winter months. Make an apple bird feeder and watch which birds arrive – can you identify any of them?

You will need:

An apple

An apple corer

Sunflowers seeds

A long piece of string

A couple of thin twigs

Birds also need clean water, so if you have a little dish you could fill it with water and put that out for them too.

1 Ask an adult to make a hole through the middle of your apple with the apple corer.

2 Make your apple nice and spiky by pushing lots of sunflower seeds into the skin of the apple.

3 Make a cross with your sticks and tie together. Then thread your string through the hole in the apple and tie the bottom end to your twigs. These make perches for the birds.

4 Find somewhere outdoors to hang your feeder – somewhere you can watch it without disturbing any birds that visit.

In spring plant some natural bird feeders like sunflowers and, by late summer, the sunflower heads will be bursting with seeds.

31

Animal tracking

Footprints are a great way to identify what wildlife is on the move when you're not watching. Here's how to make a footprint trap.

You will need:

A shallow tray (an old baking tray will do nicely)

Sand

Water

Ruler

A small dish of bait (mealworms, wet cat or dog food)

Crow

Squirrel

1 Fill the baking tray with sand and pour in water a little at a time, mixing as you go.

2 When your sand is like the type you build sandcastles with, smooth it out with a ruler.

3 Test your sand to make sure your fingers leave a mark.

4 Place your dish of bait in the middle of your tray.

5 Leave outside overnight and check for footprints in the morning.

Cat

Can you identify the footprints of any curious creatures that visit your sand pit?

BAIT

Hedgehog

Fox

Build a light trap

Many moths and other flying insects are active at nighttime. Set up a light trap to see who visits after dark.

You will need:

Pegs

White sheet

Torch

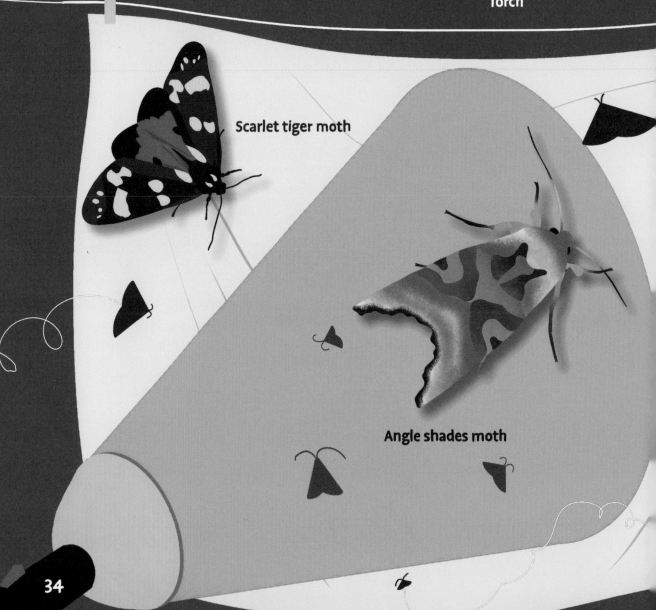

Scarlet tiger moth

Angle shades moth

1 Peg an old white sheet to a washing line or drape over a branch or fence.

2 Turn off nearby lights and switch on your bright torch.

3 Shine your light onto the sheet and wait to see who flutters in.

Poplar hawk-moth

Or from inside, shine a bright light close to a closed window. Watch as moths attracted to the light land on the outside of the window.

First published by the Natural History Museum,
Cromwell Road, London SW7 5BD
© The Trustees of the Natural History Museum,
London, 2023
Illustrations © Alistair Simmonds

A catalogue record for this book is available
from the British Library.

ISBN 978 0 565 09521 5

10 9 8 7 6 5 4 3 2 1

Internal design by Bobby Birchall, Bobby&Co
Reproduction by Saxon Digital Services
Printed in China by Toppan Leefung Limited